AN
EASY-READ
FACT
BOOK

BMX Bikes

Michael Jay

Franklin Watts

London   New York   Toronto   Sydney

Safety note
"BMX" bicycle riding can be
dangerous. Always ride with a
helmet and other recommended
safety equipment.

© 1985 Franklin Watts Ltd

First published in Great Britain
  1985 by
Franklin Watts Ltd
12a Golden Square
London W1

First published in the USA by
Franklin Watts Inc.
387 Park Avenue South
New York
N.Y. 10016

UK ISBN: 0 86313 219 7
US ISBN: 0-531-04943-4
Library of Congress Catalog Card
  Number: 84-51997

Illustrated by
Rob Burns
Hayward Art Group
Michael Roffe

Photographs supplied by
Daily Express
Richard Francis
David Jefferis

Designed and produced by
David Jefferis

Technical consultant
Richard Francis

Printed in Great Britain by
Cambus Litho, East Kilbride

BMX Bikes

Contents

BMX: bicycle motocross

▽Here you see a group of riders in a BMX race. There are normally eight riders in each heat, or "moto." The action lasts for about 30–40 seconds.

Bicycle motocross started in the United States of America in the early 1970s. It spread from California to the rest of the US, and is now popular in Britain, Europe, Australia and South Africa.

Racing is one part of BMX, freestyle the other, with most riders doing some

of each. Freestyling is the art of making the bike do tricks, some of which look almost impossible!

Later in this book, you can see how BMX riders learn to do some of the basic freestyle stunts.

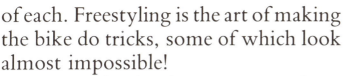

△A freestyling rider twisting his handlebars in mid-jump.

BMX racer

BMX bikes have to be strongly made to withstand the bumps and bangs of racing and stunting. The bike shown here is a typical BMX machine, with features found on most bikes.

The wheels have spokes. These are lightweight and are most suitable for racing. Freestyling bikes are best equipped with heavy but stronger nylon wheels. Different tires are used for different action. Knobby treads are best on loose gravel, smoother treads for riding on concrete or pavement.

1 Wheels can be made of alloy steel or nylon.
2 Tires are made in many different colors and come with various tread patterns.
3 Plastic saddle.
4 Adjustable seat clamp.
5 Cushioned rad pad protects rider from scrapes on cycle parts.
6 Chrome-molybdenum handlebars. "Chrome moly" is material similar to lightweight aircraft tubing.
7 Four-bolt stem clamp joins handlebars to bike.
8 Front brakes, essential for road use.
9 Chain sprocket. Different sizes give different gear ratios.
10 Chrome moly crank. Longer cranks give better acceleration.
11 Platform pedals have small studs for sure grip.

Neat stuff

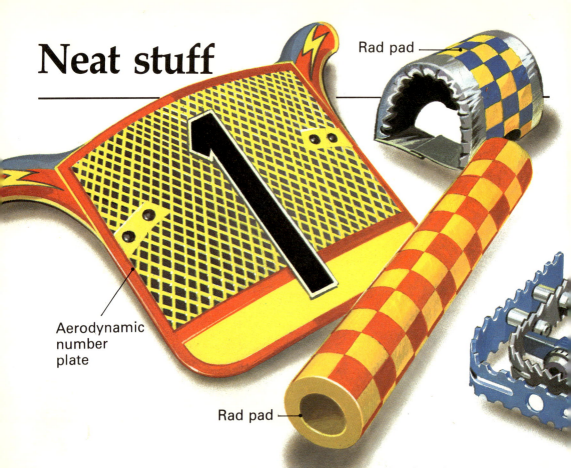

Rad pad

Aerodynamic
number
plate

Rad pad

△Here you see a selection of BMX bike accessories. There are literally hundreds of manufacturers making thousands of items of equipment.

BMX equipment is colorful and slick. Like the bikes, there are many manufacturers making a huge range of accessories.

Rad pads clip round top tubes and stem clamps. They are foam-filled to protect riders from injury if they hit the metal.

Number plates are essential in a race. The style shown in the picture is a mesh

Molded plastic handlebar grip

Studded platform pedal

△ This BMX bike has spoked wheels especially suited for racing.

design. This lets the air through, reducing wind resistance. It may not help much, but every little counts!

Platform pedals have tiny studs around the rims. They provide excellent grip for pedaling feet.

Handlebar grips come in lots of shapes and sizes. The one shown is based on aerodynamic high-speed ski-pole designs.

Safety gear

The well-prepared BMXer has to "think safety," as crashes are sometimes impossible to avoid. Wearing the right gear means that real injuries will be few, though bumps and bruises have to be expected.

The essentials for any rider include a crash helmet for head protection. A plastic mouthpiece guards the chin and nose. Colorful shirts should have thickly padded foam elbows and shoulders. Nylon trousers should be padded too, at hips, knees and shins.

Shoes are as important as the rest. Make sure you get a pair that have good grip and flexible soles.

Gloves come in many styles and materials, but old-fashioned leather gives the best all-round protection.

Always wear gloves even in practice sessions. Protect your hands whenever you ride.

▷The BMX look can be expensive. Between them, these two riders are wearing clothing worth over $400. But for serious BMX riding the right gear is essential.

10

Riders ready!

△ Eight riders line up for each moto. At bigger race meetings, start lights can be used. Red and amber lights count down to the green "go" signal.

The most important part of a BMX race is the start. Getting the lead in the first few seconds – the holeshot – and then holding on to it is the secret of successful BMX racing.

It is a good idea to listen to the starter's timing as he says, "Riders ready, pedals ready, go!" When it is your turn to race, you might get a split-second advantage as the gate drops. The gate is a small ramp sticking up at the start line. On the word "go," it drops flat, allowing the BMXers to ride over it.

The rider leading through the first berm, or banked bend, can often control the race by clever tactics. For example, a foot hanging out can block the passing line for riders behind.

▽This banked bend is called a berm, a word borrowed from motorcycle motocross. A good berm allows a rider to hit it at high speed, rounding the bend without slowing down.

Track action

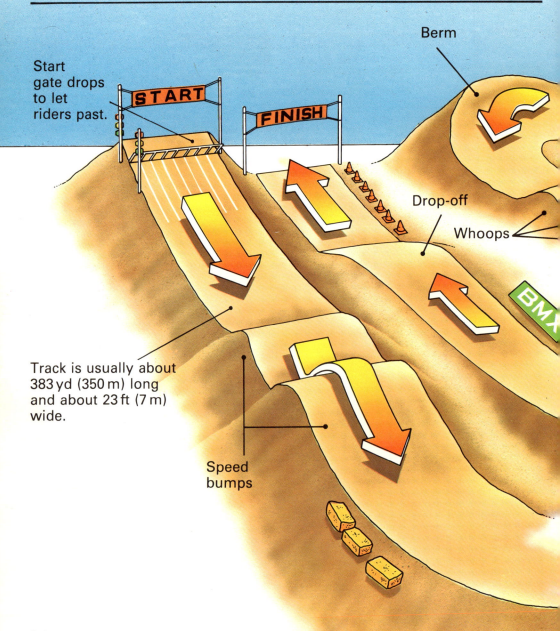

Berm

Start gate drops to let riders past.

START

FINISH

Drop-off

Whoops

BMX

Track is usually about 383 yd (350 m) long and about 23 ft (7 m) wide.

Speed bumps

Here you see a typical BMX racing track. Each course has a variety of berms, jumps and other obstacles for the riders to race on. The start is raised several feet to allow the riders a high-speed downhill start.

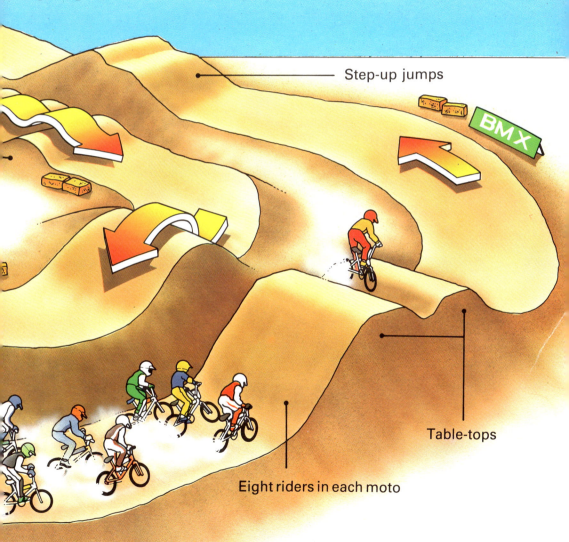

Step-up jumps

BMX

Table-tops

Eight riders in each moto

15

Secrets of success

△Grabbing air through jumps. It looks exciting, but wastes precious seconds.

Muscle power and fitness are most important in a race, but skilled tactics help too.

The leader through a berm tries to hold a midway line. Here speeds are highest, and there is little or no room for riders to squeeze by on the inside. The only way to overtake is to go up on the outside, then to move ahead of the leader.

Each BMX track is different, so tactics have to be changed from track to track. Riders can judge the right tactics for racing after they have completed a few practice races to check out the track.

Flying over jumps looks exciting to onlookers, but is the easiest way to lose a race. If you are in the air, you are not pedaling, so the bike is slowing down. Skilled riders keep the back wheel turning in the dirt as long as possible.

▽ Crashes like this can occur at a BMX race. But, when equipped with proper protective gear, riders can prevent injuries but they will usually lose the race.

Freestyle

△It is important to remember that difficult stunts should only be tried by experienced riders.

This is a kickturn on a quarterpipe, a ramp, curved like a quarter of a circle.

Freestyle is the art of stunt riding. There are lots of tricks to learn, and all need lots of practice.

Learn one trick at a time, perfecting it before you try a new one. Start off with ground stunts such as wheelies and kickturns. Later you could go on to more difficult stunts such as aerials. These are mid-air stunts that need ramps to get you launched.

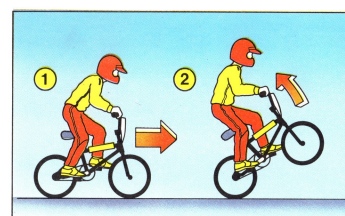

Wheelie
1 Ride forward at medium speed.
2 Lean back slightly, pull back on the bars to lift the front wheel off the ground. Sit down, balancing with the back brake.

Kickturn
Use a smooth natural mound to practice this stunt.
1 Ride forward at medium speed.
2 Climb the mound nearly up to the top.

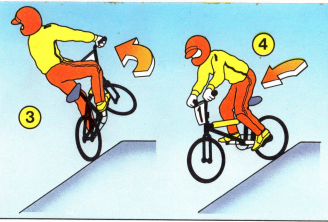

3 As you near the top, pull back on the bars.
4 Now the bike should have stopped its forward motion. Pull hard on the bars, twisting your body sideways. Keep twisting until you have turned completely around. Then ride back down the mound.

Pogo and sidewalk

△This picture shows a pogo competition, following the line of traffic cones. This is good practice for learning first-class bike control.

These two freestyle tricks are quite difficult to perfect. Both need lots of work from your arms and shoulders.

The pogo is a bouncing movement on one wheel, hopping along with each bounce. Pogos can be either front- or rear-wheel stunts. Both need a fine sense of balance.

Sidewalking means hopping the bike sideways, both wheels off the ground. A variation you can try is the snake-walk. This is also a sideways movement, but changing from front to back wheels to produce a zig-zag snaking motion.

With these tricks, like all the others, remember to wear proper protective gear, especially gloves and helmet. You could fall off lots of times before you finally master the stunts.

If a stunt goes badly wrong, don't be afraid to let go of the bike. A bent handlebar is better than an injury.

Rear-wheel pogo

1 Stand behind the bike and apply the back brake. Pull the front wheel off the ground.

2 Stand on level pedals. Pull hard on the bars, lifting the bike up and back.

3 You should be able to heave it off the ground to pogo backward. Try to keep this going.

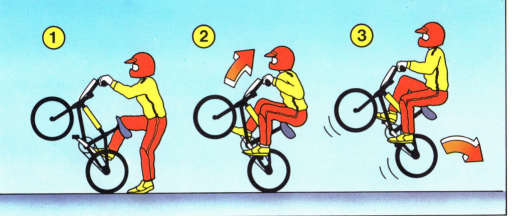

Sidewalk

1 Roll your bike to a stop.
2 Keep your balance.
3 Pull the bike up and sideways, aiming to "walk" the bike 12 in (30 cm) or so for each jump.

4 Repeat four more times. Then you can follow up with a zig-zag snakewalk.

Bunnyhops, barhops

△ This is ace BMXer Dave Sanderson. He is bunnyhopping clear over Barry Sheene's Suzuki Grand Prix motorbike.

Bunnyhops get you over obstacles without needing a takeoff ramp. The world record height is 46 in (116.8 cm) but don't expect to get near that!

Barhops look very slick and are equally difficult. Make sure you take off the number plate before starting.

22

Bunnyhop

An old milk crate or straw bale can act as an obstacle.

1 Riding toward the obstacle the rider keeps his weight over the middle of the bike.

2 The rider then lifts up the front wheel.

3 When the wheel is over the obstacle the rider pushes forward and flicks the back wheel up. He aims to land with both wheels level.

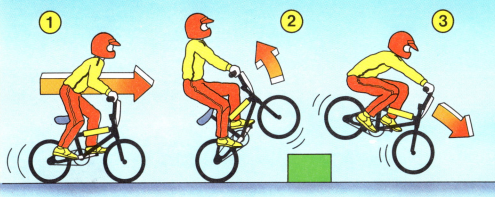

Barhop

1 Riding at a medium speed the rider swings his feet up to the crossbar.

2 Next he brings his knees up over the handlebars, without leaning too far forward.

3 The rider then sits on the crossbrace with his feet sticking out away from the front wheel.

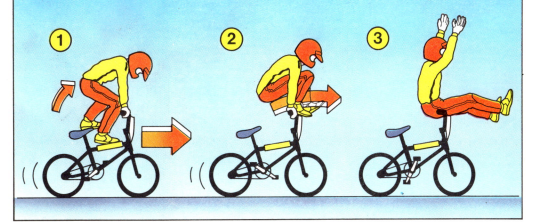

Cruisers

Cruisers are bigger bikes for older riders. At present, cruiser racing is for 14 year olds and up, but an 11-year-old class is to be introduced.

Cruiser bikes look similar to standard BMX machines, but are different in several ways. Wheels are 24 in (61 cm) in diameter, 4 in (10 cm) bigger than those of a normal BMX bike. The cruiser frame is slightly taller and the seat tube has an extra inch or two.

Like the rest of the BMX world, cruiser bike design is constantly changing and improving. One radical idea comes aboard the American Locomotion Super Cruiser.

This has two gear speeds instead of the single speed usual with BMX bikes. To ride along in low first gear, the rider pedals *forward*. To get into high-speed second gear, the rider pedals *backward*. It sounds weird but it works!

▽Cruisers in a race. The tall frame makes some things easier than on smaller BMX bikes. Cornering is slightly better, because it is easier to stay up on the pedals in tight corners.

Indoor racing

△ This track was built in the National Exhibition Centre, in Birmingham, England.

After the BMX races, the bumps and berms will be bulldozed to make room for another event.

Bad weather can ruin a BMX track or wash out an event. Dark winter nights can make meetings difficult too. An answer to these problems is the indoor track.

Indoor races are usually big events, run in stadiums otherwise used for concerts or exhibitions. The tracks are specially designed, with no risk that shaped berms will be wrecked by a sudden storm. Indoor tracks are

△ Freestyle happens indoors too. Here you see a quarterpipe aerial.

shorter than outdoor ones, well under 273 yd (250 m). The shorter runs tend to favor quick starts and fast races.

All sorts of electronic equipment can be used indoors, such as computerized lap-timer displays.

There can be drawbacks to indoor racing however. One summer race in Dijon, France, was a sweaty event. The temperature under the glass roof reached a sizzling 103°F (39°C)!

Keep rolling

Good bike maintenance is vital. Nothing is worse than dropping out of a race or ruining a freestyle trick because a badly cared-for part fails.

Keep a full tool kit at home when you can work for hours at a time. When you are out racing, make sure you take an emergency tool set.

A full set of wrenches should fit every nut and bolt on the bike. Don't try and make do with "near enough" sizes. Ill-fitting wrenches will ruin the nuts.

Pliers, screwdrivers and a pedal wrench should all be aboard too. If you are riding spoked wheels, take some spare spokes together with the equipment to mount them. You never know when you might need to fit a replacement. Tube punctures are a BMXer's nightmare. So make sure your kit includes a tube puncture repair kit, with tire levers and a pump.

△Bike shops sell basic tool kits like this, complete with bag. But you always need to add special tools and equipment to suit your particular machine.

▷This well-prepared BMXer is using a pre-race rolling road. On this, the free-running qualities of the gears and wheels can be checked as well as brakes and general balance of the bike.

BMX dictionary

Here are some popular words and jargon used in the world of BMX.

Aerial
Any mid-air freestyle trick, such as a quarterpipe aerial.

Berm
Banked curve on a BMX track. A berm comes in various designs, such as the bowl-shaped saucer berm.

Berm warfare
Name for tactics used for passing on berms.

Drop-off
The obstacle before the finishing straight. Usually has a one-yard drop, the off-ramp set at a 45 degree angle.

Endo
Front-wheel balancing trick. A curb endo uses sidewalk slabs as a brake. Make sure there is no traffic about when you practice this one.

Holeshot
Getting the lead position in the first few seconds of a race.

Moto
Heat of a BMX race.

Pegs
Axle extensions that poke out either side of the bike. Can be used on front or rear wheel or both. Used as foot stands for various freestyle tricks.

Pogo
Hopping along on the front or rear wheel.

Quarterpipe
Ramp, shaped as a quarter section of a circle. Used to get air for aerial tricks.

Radical (Rad)
Ace, plain crazy, high fashion.

Rad pad
Protective foam pad mounted on crossbar, top tube and stem clamp.

Sidewalk
Sideways hopping trick.

Snakewalk
Sideways zig-zag trick.

Speed jump
Racing trick to allow riders to pedal through jumps instead of flying in the air. The trick is to wheelie a moment before the jump, dropping the front wheel in time to keep the back wheel in the dirt.

Step-up jump
Two-stage track obstacle. One medium-height jump leads immediately to another, higher one.

Table-top
Jump on a BMX track with a flat top. Can also be a freestyle aerial trick.

The aim is to lay the bike as flat as possible at the top of a mid-air leap.

Tech Inspector
Person who checks out BMX machines for race-readiness before a moto.

Vert
Vertical. The angle you want to take off from the top of a quarterpipe.

Wheelie
Riding a bike while balanced on the back wheel. The world record wheelie lasted over *four hours*!

Whoops
Two to four mini-bumps laid about 6–10 ft (2–3 m) apart. About 20 in (50 cm) high, the jump is designed like a roller-coaster.

Other jumps include humpy Camels and giant King Kongs.

Wire
If you have a trick wired, then you can do it properly.

△Here groups of BMXers wait for their moto at a BMX meeting. Riders start young but keep going for some time. The oldest BMXers are in their late thirties.

31

Index